Why Free Speech Matters

WHY FREE SPEECH MATTERS

JAMIE WHYTE

Institute of
Economic Affairs

First published in Great Britain in 2021 by
The Institute of Economic Affairs
2 Lord North Street
Westminster
London SW1P 3LB
in association with London Publishing Partnership Ltd
www.londonpublishingpartnership.co.uk

The mission of the Institute of Economic Affairs is to improve understanding
of the fundamental institutions of a free society by analysing and expounding
the role of markets in solving economic and social problems.

A CIP catalogue record for this book is available from the British Library.

ISBN 978-0-255-36806-3

Many IEA publications are translated into languages other
than English or are reprinted. Permission to translate or to reprint
should be sought from the Director General at the address above.

Typeset in Kepler by T&T Productions Ltd
www.tandtproductions.com

Printed and bound by Hobbs the Printers Ltd

CONTENTS

THE AUTHOR

Jamie Whyte writes about economics and philosophy, especially as they relate to public policy. Until 2019 he was Research Director at the Institute of Economic Affairs. In 2014 he was leader of the ACT Party of New Zealand, a position he resigned upon failing to be elected to parliament. He has previously worked as a management consultant for Oliver Wyman and as a philosophy lecturer at Cambridge University. Jamie is the author of *Quack Policy* (2013), *Free Thoughts* (2012), *A Load of Blair* (2005) and *Crimes Against Logic* (2004). He has published more than 200 opinion columns in newspapers including *The Wall Street Journal*, *The Financial Times* and *The Times*. He won the Bastiat Prize for Economic Journalism in 2006 and was runner-up in 2010 and 2016.

SUMMARY

- Politicians and activists seek to further limit the right to free speech by extending hate speech laws and placing new legal constraints on the speech that can be posted on social media platforms.
- The Online Safety Bill is now before the UK parliament and several American politicians, including President Biden and former President Trump, have called for the revision or abolition of Section 230 of the Communications Decency Act (1996), which protects social media companies from being treated as publishers.
- Those who prize free speech must once again defend it. The central task of any defence of free speech is to explain why some limitations on speech, such as prohibitions on inciting crime and on fraud, are justified while others, such as those banning heresy or the expression of offensive ideas, are not.
- This short book argues that restrictions on speech are warranted only if they prevent harm without interfering with the primary means by which speech benefits society: namely, promoting the growth of knowledge and providing a bulwark against tyranny.

- The familiar and uncontroversial legal restrictions on speech – perjury, fraud and incitement to crime – pass this test. They do not impede the acquisition of knowledge. Nor do they prevent the powerful from being held to account. Laws against defamation are a borderline case.
- Laws aimed at preventing the expression of ideas deemed dangerous (for example, because they might increase the chance of racist murder) do not pass the test. Important new ideas are often considered dangerous. Banning their expression will inhibit the growth of knowledge. And politicians will use the power to ban the expression of dangerous ideas to protect their own power.
- Laws aimed at protecting people from being offended also fail the test. Important new ideas are often offensive to people whose worldview they challenge. Prohibitions on offensive speech thus inhibit the growth of knowledge. And ideas that challenge those in power can also be offensive, meaning that restrictions on offensive speech can be used to protect the powerful.
- Offence is not, in any case, the social harm it is taken to be, because many people enjoy being offended. They are offence masochists.
- No law that prohibits speech merely on the basis of the idea expressed can pass the test proposed in this book. So no such law should be passed. This is a simple 'limiting principle' that should guide legislators and judges.

- This principle must be applied without compromise. Politicians and bureaucrats cannot be trusted to exercise any discretion. In the absence of a rigidly applied limiting principle, politicians are placed at the top of a slippery slope of speech restrictions that self-interest gives them reason to slide down.

1   THE JOB AT HAND

Many years ago, I was taken for lunch by a prominent fig-
ure in the London free-market think tank scene. Between
courses I asked him what he thought was so good about
liberty. 'Well, it's liberty, isn't it?', he replied.

It was an impressively economical answer. Nevertheless, I didn't find it entirely satisfactory. I doubted it would
convince someone who wasn't already a fan of liberty. Nor
would it help anyone to identify the proper limits of personal freedom. Even the most ardent libertarian doesn't
think people should be allowed to do absolutely anything
they want. Libertarians don't favour legalising murder.

The kind of answer I was looking for would have told
me not only what is so good about liberty but also why
making some exceptions, such as prohibiting murder, is a
good idea. The correct answer to the question 'what's so
good about drinking?' – namely, that it is enjoyable – also
explains why you shouldn't drink all the time.

I have since come to know my pithy lunch companion
quite well. As it turns out, he could have given me a serious answer to my question. I suspect he didn't because he
thought a lovely lunch wasn't the occasion for making the
case for liberty. But life isn't just one great big lovely lunch.

Sometimes the case for liberty does need to be made. And this is one of those occasions.

Over recent decades, growing concern about the harm that words can do has eroded commitment to freedom of speech. Words are dangerous. Not only does hearing bad ideas cause people to do bad things, but words can wound directly. The government properly restricts our liberty to prevent us from harming each other. Harmful speech should be no exception.

This line of thinking lies behind the UK government's Online Safety Bill, which was published in May 2021. If passed into law, this Bill will legally constrain speech even further than the UK's hate speech laws already do, since it obliges online platforms to remove 'harmful' content that is otherwise legal. In the US, Section 230 of the 1996 Communications Decency Act – which protects social media platforms from being treated as speakers or publishers – has become unpopular with those who worry about 'online harm'. And some, including President Biden, seek legislative reforms similar to the UK's Online Safety Bill.

Those of us opposed to such legislation need to make the case for free speech, again. And we need to say more than 'well, it's free speech, isn't it?'. After all, we all believe that *some* constraints on speech are justified. For example, you shouldn't be allowed to incite violence, and you shouldn't be allowed to lie when entering into contractual agreements. We need an answer to the question 'What's so good about free speech?' that can also tell us why some exceptions are warranted, and why others are not.

That's what this book attempts to do. I argue that what is so good about free speech is not that it is an inalienable natural right or essential for human dignity or anything else metaphysical or otherwise mysterious. Rather, free speech is so good because it benefits us so much. And it benefits us in two main ways: by helping to advance knowledge and by providing a bulwark against tyranny. The justifiable limits to free speech are those that prevent harm without impeding the provision of these two benefits. That's why a prohibition on inciting violence is justified but hate speech laws and the Online Safety Bill are not. Defamation is a borderline case.

Before making this argument, however, I need to clarify what I mean by 'free speech'. What is it that I am defending?

2   WHAT IS FREE SPEECH?

An interaction that must occur thousands of times a day on social media goes like this. Jack says something that Jill objects to – that women don't have penises, let's suppose.[1] Jack objects to Jill's objection on the ground that he has a right to express his opinions. 'You do indeed,' replies Jill, 'but I also have a right to express my opinion that what you said is objectionable. Free speech does not protect you from criticism.'

Jill is right. In fact, a law that protected people from criticism would severely constrain speech. Nor is free speech a protection from losing friends or being shunned by polite society when you say something people don't like. Free speech does not mean that speech can have no ill consequences for the speaker. The 'free' in 'free speech' does not mean 'comes at no cost'.

A right to free speech protects you from one particular cost of speech: namely, being punished by the authorities. If Jack's wife leaves him because he tweeted that women

---

1   Some may think this is a silly example. It isn't. In 2018, feminists who had put up stickers saying 'women don't have penises' were investigated by the Merseyside police. This is the kind of statement that some authorities now believe to be sufficiently harmful to warrant legal intervention.

don't have penises, she has not violated his freedom of speech. If the police come and arrest him, they have. In Iran, insulting Islam is illegal. Iranians do not enjoy free speech – at least, not on religious matters. And in countries such as Russia and China, where criticising the government can land you in prison, people do not have free speech on political matters.

Free speech is a protection against the state and its coercive powers. No such protection is needed against your fellow citizens because they are already prohibited from using coercive power over you. If Jack's wife locks him in the bathroom for a month to punish him for his dreadful comment, she is breaking the law whether or not Jack has a right to say whatever he wants. Or, to put it another way, it is the crime of wrongful imprisonment, not his right to free speech, that protects Jack from being locked in the bathroom by his wife. All the legal ways in which ordinary people may 'punish' Jack for what he says are things they are free to do in any event. No one is obliged to be anyone's wife or to invite them to dinner parties or to follow them on Twitter.

Free speech is like free trade. Ruby grows potatoes on her farm. Each Saturday, she loads them onto her truck and drives them to the nearby farmer's market where she offers them for sale. Ron drives to the market to do his weekly food shopping. He likes the look of Ruby's potatoes and buys 10 pounds of them for £10. This is free trade. But it doesn't mean Ruby will suffer no cost if she produces potatoes people don't like. On the contrary, she will ultimately go broke. In this sense, Ruby's commercial conduct is regulated. But it is regulated by 'the market': that is, by the preferences of consumers. The sense in which the trade remains free is that the government has not used its coercive powers to dictate the terms of the trade (let's implausibly imagine): it hasn't specified the required size of the potatoes or how they must be grown or how they must be packaged or the price at which Ruby must sell them or anything else. Nor does it protect Ruby from going broke by subsidising her or bailing her out when in financial trouble. Nor does it prevent others from growing potatoes and competing with Ruby. That's what we mean by 'free trade'. And we mean the same thing by 'free speech'. Speakers are disciplined only by their audience, and not by the authorities. Speakers face social constraints, not legal constraints.

Here is a slight complication that causes more confusion than it should. The owner of the farmers' market may impose all the rules that, in our imaginary free trade world, the government has not imposed. And even if he doesn't impose exactly the kinds of rules I mentioned above, he will certainly impose *some* rules. He won't allow just anyone to open a stall selling just anything. He won't let a pornographer set up shop next to a sweet stall. Surely, then, we do not have free trade at the farmers' market.

Yes we do. Because the owner of the market is but another voluntary participant in the trading process, and his market is but another product that faces market disciplines. The rules of his market are part of what will attract or repel sellers and buyers who might use it. The rules are a feature of his product. Markets compete for customers, just as the businesses who operate in them do. Unilever lists its shares on the London Stock Exchange, but it needn't. It could list them on the New York Stock Exchange or on one of the many other stock exchanges around the world. My daughter sells her unwanted clothes through depop.com, but she needn't. If she preferred, she could sell them through Carousell. Provided the government does not impose markets' rules on them, we have a free market in markets and a free market in the goods traded through those markets.

This is why the content rules imposed by online platforms where people speak are not limitations on free speech. They are part of each platform's product offering and a basis on which they compete for users. Provided governments do not dictate their content rules, we have a free market in online speech platforms and a free market in the speech 'traded' through them. The same goes for universities and the student organisations within them. Their speech rules are product features that will attract or repel students. Provided they can adopt any rules they choose and no one is forced to attend or join them, their rules do not diminish freedom of speech. The same also goes for employers who fire employees for violations of speech rules. Company speech rules are simply another part of the package of employment conditions that employers use to attract employees. No one is forced to work for any particular employer. If an employer's speech rules are too strict, he will find himself having to increase wages to attract willing staff of a given quality, as he will if they are too lax.

But what if no online platform will host your speech? Surely then you do not have free speech. Yes you do. A free market in goods still exists even when no shop is willing to stock someone's product. A legal obligation to stock a product would violate free trade. A universal voluntary refusal to do so does not. Similarly, free speech still exists even when every online platform refuses to provide an account to someone who posts things they don't want on their site. Your right to free speech does not oblige anyone to give you a platform from which others can hear what you have to say. Twitter is no more obliged to give you a Twitter account than the *Wall Street Journal* is obliged to give you a weekly column.[2]

By adopting this narrow conception of free speech, by seeing it as something constrained only when speech is punished by governments, many will think I am missing the biggest threat to it. Yes, they will say, legislation such as the Online Safety Bill is a problem. But the big problem is cultural, not legal. It is not the law that chills the free exchange of ideas so much as the censorious mood of our age: the Twitter pile-ons, the lost jobs, the lost friends. In short, the cancel culture.

---

2 US courts have interpreted the First Amendment to the Constitution, which protects Americans' right to free speech, as preventing the government from compelling a person to pay for someone else's speech. Some have argued that an exception should be made for online platforms. They should be obliged to host all legal speech because, like telephone infrastructure suppliers, they are properly regarded as 'common carriers'. Explaining why they are wrong would take me too far from the central thread of this chapter (but see Feeney 2021).

This was John Stuart Mill's position in *On Liberty*. He was more worried about 'society' and its intolerance towards free thinkers than about the legal restrictions on speech. I sympathise, not only with Mill, who confronted the intolerant moralism of mid-nineteenth-century England, but with those who nowadays confront a new intolerant moralism, one concerned not with Christian virtue but with respect for 'identity' – that is to say, with race, gender and sexuality, among a growing list of sacred characteristics. And I do not doubt that cancel culture stifles speech.

But what can be done about it?

Consider Hank, who lives in Nalem, a tiny town in New England. Hank enjoys all of America's First Amendment protections of his freedom to speak but, whereas Hank is a polyamorous atheist, everyone else in Nalem is a puritanical Christian. If Hank said what he really thinks about most moral issues, he'd have no friends. Indeed, he might lose his job at Nalem Tax Advisors, having signed an employment contract that allows the owner to fire him if he says anything that damages the firm's standing in the community. So he keeps his mouth shut.

How should this social stifling of Hank's speech be overcome? Should the law oblige the other residents of Nalem to be friendly with Hank even when they disapprove of the things he says? Should they be required to invite him to barbeques and bring him gifts on his birthday? Should employment contracts such as the one Hank freely entered be proscribed? There is no acceptable legal solution to Hank's problem. If he wants to stay in Nalem and to speak more freely, he will need to convince his neighbours to be more tolerant.

Many readers who live in Britain or in American towns less puritanical than Nalem will share Hank's problem, if not his particular reasons for it. Even if the law properly protects your freedom to speak, you may still be stifled by social constraints. Like Hank, you may have a culture war to fight.

You won't need to start it. The war already rages. Resistance to cancel culture abounds, and private-sector remedies have sprung up. The social media platform Parler was established in 2018 as a response to censorship on Twitter and Facebook. GB News, an explicitly pro–free speech television news network, has just been launched in the UK. Several talk radio show hosts consistently rail against cancel culture. And every week you can read several opinion columns complaining about the censoriousness of the 'woke left'. Nor is the resistance all talk. Get cancelled and the Free Speech Union will come to your aid.[3]

Such responses are heartening. But they don't help me to answer the question of this book: namely, which speech should the law prohibit? No one serious believes the answer is 'none'. Everyone favours free speech 'within limits'. What then are those limits? What is the difference between justified speech prohibitions, such as those on fraud and incitement to murder, and unjustified ones,

---

3 The journalist Toby Young, who lost jobs in 2018 because of old tweets about women's breasts, founded the Free Speech Union in 2020. The Union takes action on behalf of subscribers who fall victim to cancel culture.

such as denying the existence of Allah? This is the serious question in the debate about free speech. Bemoaning the creeps who try to get people fired for saying things the creeps don't like would contribute nothing to answering it. And, anyway, my bemoaning would only be lost in the ocean of bemoaning.

So let's get on with the work of the book, which starts with understanding what is so good about free speech.

3 ADVANCING KNOWLEDGE

A little over two hundred years ago, economic growth in The Netherlands and Britain started to take off, as it did soon after in most of Europe and in North America. In the UK in 1800, gross domestic product per person was £2,000 a year (in 2021 money), having been only a little lower a thousand years earlier. By 1900, it had risen to £5,000. Today it is £32,000. The gains in human welfare have been astounding. Even relatively poor Britons today enjoy a quality of life that the aristocracy of 1800 could not have imagined. They drive cars, watch films on their phones, surf the net, take food from the refrigerator and heat it in the microwave, survive once-deadly diseases with no more inconvenience than taking a course of antibiotics, and have pain-free dentistry, among many other modern wonders.

This extraordinary progress is explained by the explosion of innovation that began in the late eighteenth century and has not stopped since. In other words, it has been caused by an explosion of good ideas. People started thinking of new and better ways of making things – most obviously, by replacing manual production with mechanised production powered by fossil fuels. And they started thinking of new and better things to make, such as trains and electric lighting and planes and telephones and penicillin and computers and lycra-cotton leggings and so on and on and on.

Why did innovation take off in Britain in the late eighteenth century? Scholars offer a variety of answers (see, for example, Mokyr 2017; McCloskey 2017; Davies 2019). But economic liberty is part of all the serious ones, including Karl Marx's answer. Unlike economically sclerotic Qing Dynasty China, the law and the monarch allowed profit-seekers to invest in any new production techniques and new products that took their fancy. Governmental authority played a minimal role in determining which goods were produced, by whom, or how.

Another part of the answer is the rapid progress of science that had begun in Europe in the seventeenth century. The new techniques and products of the industrial revolution drew on the new knowledge provided by the scientific revolution. And, as with the industrial revolution, the scientific revolution occurred, in part, because the role of authority had been minimised. Knowledge of the natural world was no longer taken to come from revelation but from confronting theories with observed reality. How do you know whether the sun orbits the earth or vice versa? Not by consulting scripture but by seeing which theory best accounts for our observations of the night sky, the movement of the tides, and so on.

Authority in the field of belief had stifled the expression of ideas contrary to religious dogma. It had thereby inhibited the production of new ideas, not only directly but indirectly. For, as Matt Ridley has memorably put it, innovation comes from 'ideas having sex' (Ridley 2020). If ideas aren't allowed out, they cannot meet, make love, and have children. It is no surprise that intellectual progress in Europe had been so feeble in the censorious centuries before the rebellion against the authority of the Catholic Church.

In his *Kindly Inquisitors*, Jonathan Rauch calls the modern anti-authoritarian approach to the acquisition of knowledge 'liberal science'. Its defining characteristic is that 'no one gets the final say' about what is true (Rauch 1993: 46). Liberal science is decentralised and egalitarian, in the sense that no one is special. It is irrelevant *who* advances a theory. All that matters is how well the theory accounts for the observations it is supposed to explain. There is no place for authority when it comes to discovering the truth.

A theory might have done well in its confrontations with observation, but that doesn't mean it cannot be improved upon. In 1905, Newtonian (or classical) physics was the exemplar of a successful scientific theory, not only confirmed by the results of many experiments but the foundation of all manner of technology. Yet in that year Einstein published his special theory of relativity, which did an even better job of explaining observed phenomena than Newtonian physics did (as we discovered some years later). Under the liberal science regime of 1905, he was free to do so. If science had been controlled by the Church of Newtonian Physics or the government had banned statements that insult the genius of Newton, he might not have been allowed to, and the progress of knowledge would have been hindered.

This, then, is my basic case for free speech. It allows new ideas to be produced and tested as fast as possible, and thereby promotes the growth of knowledge and human well-being. The extraordinary progress of knowledge and well-being over the last five hundred years is founded on free speech. We should cherish it.

This was not quite but almost John Stuart Mill's reason for promoting free speech. Like John Milton before him, Mill thought that 'in a free and open encounter' between truth and falsity, truth would prevail (Milton 1644). Subsequent writers have summarised this idea by saying that truth will prevail in a free 'market for ideas'. Just as good (physical) products win out over bad products in a free market for products, true ideas will beat false ideas in a free market for ideas.

This is an unfortunate analogy. 'True' is not to the market for ideas what 'good' is to the market for products. Consider cars. BMWs are better than Fords, you might think: faster, better-handling and more beautiful. Then why have Fords not been driven from the free market for cars? The answer is that when saying BMWs are better than Fords we have forgotten to consider price. BMWs are more expensive than Fords. When that is taken into account, BMWs are no better. Both survive in the market for cars because not everyone makes the same trade-off between price and other features of cars, most obviously because not everyone is equally wealthy. The idea that only good products survive in a free market for products is close to necessarily true. The necessity arises from what it means for a product to be good: namely, that when everything (including price) is taken into account, some consumers prefer it to all their alternatives.[1]

Like cars, ideas have many qualities that might appeal to someone or might repel him. Most people would prefer their beliefs to be true, if only because true beliefs guide you more successfully through life than do false ones. But truth isn't the only thing someone might like in an idea. Being easily understood is an appealing quality in an idea. Astrology beats developmental psychology on this basis. Being fashionable in your preferred social circle is also a virtue in an idea you might believe (or say you do). This will make the idea that some women have penises attractive to many undergraduates at Cambridge University. Or an idea might suit you because it annoys your annoying parents. Or, or, or. Truth is only one feature of an idea. There is, therefore, no more reason to think that a free market for ideas will favour true ideas than to think a free market for cars will favour cars that can accelerate from 0 to 60 miles per hour in three seconds. Nor would truth be guaranteed even if the consumers of ideas sought nothing but the truth. For as behavioural economists keep telling us, and conmen have always known, we humans are inclined to

---

1   It is only close to necessarily true because various kinds of market failure can allow bad products to survive a free market. Or, in other words, they mean free markets can be inefficient. But this is irrelevant to the present point, which is that the way free markets eliminate bad products in ideal-ised circumstances (where there are no sources of market failure) does not apply to false ideas in the 'market for ideas'.

make certain intellectual errors, not only at random but in predictable ways (see, for example, Thaler and Sunstein 2008).

Some have concluded that Mill's 'argument from truth' is dead in the water. Truth will not always beat falsity in a 'free and open encounter'. Free speech – or a free market in ideas, if you must call it that – will not drive error from the field. In an article about free speech and hate speech, the political philosopher Jeffrey Howard (2019) explains why he doesn't even consider Mill's argument:

> [T]wo decades ago it would have been unthinkable to ignore the idea of an unregulated marketplace of ideas, and its importance for the discovery of truth, as a central argument for free speech, an argument with influential roots in the work of J. S. Mill. Yet ... the general empirical claim on which this model appears to rest has been thoroughly discredited.

This quick dismissal of the 'argument from truth' is based on a misunderstanding – at least of the version of the argument I am making. Free speech can fail to eliminate error, or can even encourage it, while still accelerating the growth of knowledge.

My late aunt (may she nourish Gaia) believed a lot of woo-woo: astrology, tarot readings, numerology, that kind of thing. She even believed that women of exceptional femininity could impregnate themselves, an idea that descended upon her after divorcing the supposed father of her children. But my aunt's wonky ideas didn't impede the progress of knowledge. Nor did they prevent her from enjoying the benefits of that progress. She watched television and flew to Singapore in aeroplanes, among other knowledge-based activities.

My aunt's errors and the knowledge that she did not possess but from which she benefited had a common cause: namely, free speech (or liberal science, to use Rauch's apt expression). Had the strictures of the Spanish Inquisition still applied during her lifetime, the variety and flamboyance of her errors would have been much reduced. But so would her TV watching and jetting around, since the knowledge on which these activities depend would not have been produced. Or imagine that legislators in 1900, frustrated by the persistence of religious mumbo jumbo despite the progress of science, had passed a law forbidding people to say things inconsistent with Newtonian physics. Again, my aunt's errors might have been suppressed. But so would Einstein's breakthrough.

Return to the car market analogy. Some people are in the business of producing cars that can carry four children and a dog and be driven safely by someone who is nervous and uncoordinated. Others are in the business of producing cars that have a chance of winning Formula One races. Similarly, some people are in the business of producing ideas that make people feel better about death and place money in the donation box. Others are in the business of producing ideas about reality and, especially, about the laws of nature – ideas that might be used to make new things or to make old things in new ways or to live differently. Consumers of these ideas are anxious that they be true, since otherwise their application will not have the desired effects: the diseases won't be cured, the bridges will collapse, the images won't turn up on the screen of the smartphone. And producers of these ideas are correspondingly anxious that they be true. They apply high standards of intellectual rigour and signal in expensive ways that they have done so. The long and arduous PhD degree process, the tedious conferences, the publication of methods and results, the peer reviewing, the ostracising of frauds: all this palaver doesn't only ensure intellectual rigour but displays it to consumers of the ideas produced. This is the part of the market for ideas that matters for human welfare. And laws that restrict what people may say can only impede its progress.

Some readers may think I am talking only about 'hard sciences' such as physics and chemistry. I am not. Ideas about constitutional arrangements have promoted peace and prosperity. Ideas about the equal dignity of all humans led to the emancipation of slaves and women. Ideas about the effect of import tariffs on domestic consumers led to the abolition of the Corn Laws and the nineteenth-century era of freer trade. It isn't only ideas from the hard sciences that can benefit mankind; it isn't only the hard sciences that can be pursued with intellectual rigour; and it isn't only the hard sciences whose contribution to human welfare is impeded by legal restrictions on what people may say.

4 PREVENTING TYRANNY

With the 'argument from truth' (wrongly) falling from favour, the most popular defence of free speech has become the 'argument from democracy'. Democracy is good. Free speech is essential for democracy. Therefore, free speech is good. That's the gist of the argument (see, for example, Heinze 2016; Warburton 2009).

Alas, the second premise is false. Democracy is rule by the people. We can have rule by the people without free speech. The people might even vote to prohibit speech. Debate would be constrained, of course, but why does constraining debate eliminate democracy? It may make democracy less effective, but that is another matter. Which suggests a better way of formulating the argument:

1. Democracy is good for achieving X.
2. Democracy would not achieve X without free speech.
3. X is good.
4. Therefore, free speech is good.

What X can we slot into premises 1, 2 and 3 that makes them true? Before getting to my preferred X – preventing tyranny – we should consider another candidate for X:

namely, that democracy causes the government to adopt good policies and pass good laws.

What makes a policy or law good? The answer cannot be that a policy is good just because it is arrived at democratically. Then premise 1 of our argument is trivially true and premise 2 is false. Free speech is surplus to requirements. Any policy arrived at by a democratic process is *ipso facto* a good one. Democracy would produce good policies whether or not free speech prevailed.

The argument requires 'good' to mean something independent of democracy. Let's suppose it means 'increases social welfare'. A policy is good if it makes the members of society altogether better off. This is vague, if only because I haven't said what 'better off' means. And some will disagree with my suggestion that good policies are ones that increase social welfare. But this vagueness and disagreement don't matter for present purposes. The idea that democracy delivers good policy is implausible on any non-trivial interpretation of 'good policy'.

Public choice theory – the economic analysis of how collective decisions are actually made, as opposed to the reassuring fantasies of the civics classroom – gives us many reasons to believe that bad policies are favoured by democratic decision-making.[1] Let's consider just the reason most relevant to free speech: namely, rational voter ignorance.

---

1 For a clear and concise introduction to public choice theory, see Butler (2012).

To understand the problem, start not with voting for politicians but with a question that arises in banking. How many people should be involved in assessing and approving a loan application? The ideal number may vary with the complexity of the application, but the right answer is always 'very few'. If a loan officer's decision required agreement from a majority of 99 other bankers, his own judgement would have little effect on the final outcome. So he would have little incentive to think hard about the application and the likelihood that the loan will be repaid. Since this would be equally true for each of the other 99 bankers, none would bother to think hard. Why struggle to make the right decision when your decision will have no effect? When the number of assessors is high, the quality of assessment is low.

This is the position of voters in a general election. Each individual's vote makes no difference to the outcome. Even marginal constituencies are won with majorities of hundreds. If you had stayed home instead of voting, the same candidate would have been elected. If each person's vote makes no difference to the outcome of the election, why do so many people bother to vote? This is the so-called 'paradox of voting' (Downs 1957). One answer, as the economist Geoffrey Brennan has argued, is that people enjoy it (Brennan and Lomasky 1993). The simple act of going to a polling booth and ticking a box is felt to display democratic virtue. And, by ticking one box rather than another, people can feel themselves to be generous or pragmatic or progressive or something else they like to be.

Enjoying such feelings is easily worth the cost of taking a few hours off work every few years. But it isn't worth the effort of learning a lot about economics, jurisprudence, international relations or even the policies of the candidate you vote for. And the facts support this theory. Research into voters' knowledge reveals a stunning degree of ignorance. Most would be as likely to vote for the best candidate if they entered the polling booth blindfolded.

In fact, blindfolds would increase most voters' chance of making the best choice. Because, as Bryan Caplan has shown, ignorant voters do not make their mistakes randomly. They are biased towards particular errors (Caplan 2008).[2] Hence the many foolish policies followed by democratic governments. And hence politicians' sentimental and grandiose rhetoric. Modern politics is just as you should expect it to be when votes are cast by (rationally) ignorant people taking advantage of a low-cost source of emotional gratification. And all this goes on in America, where free speech has stronger legal protection than in any other country. No one who has witnessed a Republican or Democrat political rally can believe that free speech guarantees high intellectual standards in politics.

In the previous chapter I argued that the 'argument from advancing knowledge' is not undermined by the

---

2   Condorcet (1785) claimed that a small minority of informed voters sufficed to bring about the right result in a democracy. The ignorant majority would allocate their votes randomly (and thus evenly) across the alternatives, and the result would depend solely on the way the informed minority voted. Caplan shows that this is too optimistic, because the allocation of ignorant votes is not in fact random.

fact that free speech does not prevent widespread error. The progress of knowledge depends on the activities of an intellectual elite. Provided serious thinkers are free to do their thing, knowledge will progress. But democracy is, by design, a mass activity. In a democracy, widespread error leads to the victory of bad policy. Free speech only makes this more likely because voters are ignorant and easily convinced by bogus appeals to their erroneous biases.

This might look like an argument against democracy or, at least, an argument against free speech in democracies. Perhaps a committee of wise people should decide which ideas are too dangerously wrong for voters to hear. As we will see in chapter 6, serious intellectuals are now making this argument. But it is a bad argument because it misunderstands the role of democracy in giving us good government. Democracy is not a device for policy optimisation. It is not a way of ensuring we get the best possible policies. It is a way of making sure that we do not get the worst possible government.

Throughout history, governments have done terrible things to the populations they govern. The twentieth century alone provides many examples: the Nazi government of Germany slaughtered more than 180,000 German Jews; the Soviet government imprisoned and murdered millions of domestic political opponents; the government of apartheid-era South Africa forcibly relocated millions of black South Africans from cities to racially segregated townships. In none of these cases could the victims of the government vote against those in power.

My point is not that democratically elected governments never do terrible things. The British government was democratically elected in the 1950s when the British army was committing atrocities in Kenya. David Cameron, Barack Obama and Nicolas Sarkozy were democratically elected. That didn't stop them bombing Libya in 2011, directly killing thousands of people and unleashing violent political chaos which has devastated millions of lives, not only in Libya but across North and West Africa. These are not counter-examples to my point because Libyans can't vote in British, American or French elections, and nor could the Mau Mau insurgents who the British army tortured and summarily executed vote in British elections. Elected politicians kill and torture people, yes. But they rarely kill and torture people who can vote in the elections on which their jobs depend. When the domestic population can't vote, those in power are inclined to treat them with the same respect that democratic politicians show foreigners. Democracy is good at stopping that from happening. In other words, democracy is good at stopping domestic tyranny.

Free speech is an important part of how democracy achieves this. If the government could control what voters hear, those in power would have less reason to fear voters. The constraint that democracy places on the conduct of the powerful would be greatly reduced. Voters may be ignorant and irrational and inclined to vote for bad policies. But it doesn't follow from this that they are such suckers that they would vote for politicians who pose a tyrannical threat to them, provided this fact can be brought to their attention. That's why such politicians never emerge in stable modern democracies, all of which still enjoy near complete freedom of political speech. They don't stand a chance.

Even without democracy, freedom of speech constrains the worst tendencies of those in power. You can tell it does, because the rulers of undemocratic countries invariably impose legal constraints on political speech (or arbitrary constraints, such as murdering journalists). The rulers of undemocratic countries are still constrained by the willingness of the population to accept their rule. If things get sufficiently bad, they face the prospect of a bloody uprising in which they may well lose more than their jobs. Even without voters, rulers are threatened by a population that despises them. This gives them a strong incentive to control the information available to the population.

The ideas that threaten those in power need not be overtly political. Any idea that could significantly change the way we live threatens them. After all, they enjoy power *with things as they are now.* Why would they welcome big new ideas that threaten to shake things up? Roman Catholic clerics were hostile to Galileo's idea that the earth orbits the sun, and imprisoned him for expressing it, because it threatened the religious worldview on which their power was based. Soviet politicians stifled not only political speech critical of their regime but 'bourgeois science', theories that they took to be inconsistent with the Marxist worldview on which their power was based – or, at least, on which its legitimation was based. John Stuart

Mill thought that those who suppress the expression of ideas they don't like make the mistake of being certain that their own beliefs are true, which no one ever should be. Perhaps they sometimes do. But thinking an idea false isn't the only reason to dislike it. The powerful have reason to dislike any big new idea, especially when they fear it may be true.[3]

---

3 This is generally true, but not always. In *The Wealth Explosion*, Stephen Davies (2019) argues that the explosion of new ideas that occurred in northwest Europe in the eighteenth century was a result of the peculiar fragmentation of Europe at that time, with scores of small countries in the territory that is now Belgium, the Netherlands, Germany, Switzerland and northern Italy. The rulers of large stable countries, such as Song dynasty China, have an interest in suppressing new ideas that threaten to destabilise their rule. The rulers of small countries threatened by hostile neighbours have an interest in technological progress that can give them a military advantage. So the rulers of the little countries of eighteenth-century Europe allowed their populations the liberty required for innovation.

5 PROPER LIMITS

Free speech is good because it advances knowledge and provides a bulwark against tyranny. It may also benefit us in other ways, but these two are enough to make us prize it.[1]

Yet free speech is not an unalloyed good. The freedom to say whatever you want could be used for wrongdoing. You might use it to defraud people with whom you are doing business or to falsely accuse someone of committing a crime or to incite people to commit murder. No one thinks that valuing free speech means people should be able to say whatever they want, whenever they want to. Famously, if now tediously, you shouldn't be allowed to yell 'fire!' in a crowded theatre when it isn't on fire.

Certain restrictions on free speech are justified. Everyone serious agrees. But *which* restrictions are justified? Answering this question is the difficult part of the debate about free speech. The answer we want is not a list of allegedly justified restrictions. It is a principle by which those restrictions get onto the list.

John Stuart Mill offered such a principle in his *On Liberty* (1859):

---

1 For a sketch of other arguments for free speech, see Howard (2019).

> The only purpose for which power can be rightfully exercised over any member of a civilized community, against his will, is to prevent harm to others.

This 'harm principle', as it has come to be known, explains why the law can rightly prohibit speech that incites murder but not, according to Mill, speech that offends religious sentiments (since Mill thought that those who are merely offended are not harmed). The other uncontroversial legal restrictions on speech, such as the laws against fraud and perjury, are also justified by the harm principle. As far as I know, no other general principle for limiting freedom of speech has been proposed. All those now competing in the market for ideas are variants on Mill's harm principle.[2]

As so far stated, the harm principle would justify a prohibition on almost every action. For almost every action does some harm to others. Or, in other words, it imposes costs on others. When I walk down the street, I take up space that someone else might have liked to occupy. People see me, and some of them probably don't like the sight. But these harms don't mean I should be prohibited from walking down the street. For the prohibition is more harmful than the harms it prevents. Stopping me from leaving the house is much worse for me (and for some other people) than the suffering avoided by those who might like to occupy my space on the pavement or who would rather

---

2   Feinberg (1985) offers what he calls the 'offense principle'. He takes it to be additional to Mill's harm principle, rather than a special case of it, because, like Mill, he denies that offence is a kind of harm. But they are wrong about this, as I will argue in chapter 6.

not see me. Restrictions on liberty are justified only when they reduce total or *net* harm, including the harm done by the restrictions.

Prohibitions on speech are no exception. A law that bans a certain kind of speech may save some from harm that the speech would do. But if the prohibition prevents speech from which others would have benefited more, it causes net harm to society. The legal theorist and federal judge, Richard Posner, expressed this idea by saying that a judge should deem a speech regulation to be consistent with the First Amendment (not ruled out by it) if and only if:

$$V + E < P \times L$$

where V is the value to society of the suppressed information, E is the 'legal-error costs incurred in trying to distinguish the information that society desires to suppress from valuable information', P is the probability of harm if the speech in question is not suppressed, and L is the loss to society if that harm occurs ($P \times L$ is the 'expected loss') (Posner 1986).[3]

The uncontroversial restrictions on speech, such as the law against inciting murder, pass this cost–benefit test quite easily. Yes, the inciter may miss out on having his

---

3 'Legal-error cost' will be unfamiliar to most readers. In this context, it is the cost to society of trying to determine if any speech is net valuable or harmful. The cost comes not merely from the process of trying to determine this but from errors: mistaking net valuable speech for net harmful speech and vice versa.

target murdered, which will disappoint him. But this loss to the inciter is far smaller than the gain to his would-be victim. And the prohibition on inciting murder imposes no obvious cost on the rest of society. The prohibition is therefore net beneficial. The same goes for prohibitions on fraud and perjury. They impose a small cost on a few people who would like to indulge in them while bestowing great benefits on others. They help people in large anonymous societies to trust each other and they thereby facilitate trade and the other kinds of cooperation on which our welfare depends.

The problem with the principle that speech prohibitions should reduce net harm, and Posner's mathematical formulation of it, is not that it is wrong or inconsistent with the uncontroversial examples of justified speech restrictions. The problem is that it is trivial. As a critic of Posner's formula has put it: 'As a general thesis ... the cost–benefit statement is true by definition. It is little different from saying that the judge should always make the correct decision. The controversial step arises in the concrete application of the formula' (Hammer 1988: 510). If we are to provide guidance to American judges deciding First Amendment cases or legislators voting on laws that prohibit speech, we must offer a principle of more substance. When is the cost–benefit test for such laws likely to be passed? Or, more to the point, when is it likely to be failed?

The answer is to be found in the reasons we value free speech so highly: namely, that it advances knowledge and prevents tyranny. Prohibitions that impede speech from playing these roles will do more harm than good. This is a substantive thesis that provides a practical test for any proposed or extant restriction on speech. It is not true by necessity or definition. It is *logically possible* for a restriction on speech that inhibits free inquiry or restrains the scrutiny of our rulers to prevent more harm than it causes. But, as a matter of fact, it never would. Why am I so sure? Because the benefits of advancing knowledge and of preventing tyranny are massive and, by comparison, the harms caused by speech are tiny – as I will show in the next two chapters when considering prohibitions on expressing dangerous and offensive ideas.

This test causes no problems for the uncontroversial restrictions on speech. A law against inciting murder does not prevent scientists or other scholars from following their research wherever it leads them, from hearing ideas that might stimulate new research or from exposing the errors of others. The same is true of laws against perjury and fraud. In fact, they may facilitate the acquisition of knowledge.

The uncontroversial cases also pass the political scrutiny test. Laws against incitement, fraud and perjury do not prevent journalists or anyone else from exposing the misconduct and folly of the powerful. Defamation law may seem to fail the test. People are surely deterred from exposing the misconduct of the powerful by the threat of being sued for slander or libel. This chilling effect is reduced by the fact that the truth of the defamatory claim is always a defence. It does not entirely eliminate the chill because judges and juries sometimes make mistakes, and someone exposing misconduct will therefore always face some legal risk. But this doesn't count against my test because defamation is in fact a debatable case. Many believe that it is too easy to sue for defamation in England, and that the law should be changed to reduce the legal risk faced by those seeking to expose the misconduct of the powerful.[4] It is a virtue of my test that it explains why this borderline case is a borderline case.

Before considering recent and proposed speech laws in light of this test, it will be useful to make one final observation, an observation that allows me to convert my test for speech prohibitions into a simpler and more easily followed rule for legislators and judges.

All the uncontroversial speech laws, such as those prohibiting fraud and incitement, concern what has come to be known as *time, place and manner*. They do not impose a blanket ban on expressing certain ideas. Rather, they prohibit actions, such as defrauding people and inciting murder, which are performed by expressing certain ideas in certain circumstances. *Kill Bill* is the title of a Quentin Tarantino movie. It isn't a criminal offence, because there is no particular Bill who was being targeted by Tarantino and because no one will take movie titles as genuine recommendations for crime. But 'Kill Bill!' yelled to an angry mob assembled outside the home of William Jones, a man believed to have raped a local girl, would probably qualify as incitement to murder. It is not illegal to say that you saw

---

4   Defamation law in the UK was reformed by the Defamation Act of 2013, the aim of which was 'to reform the law of defamation to ensure that a fair balance is struck between the right to freedom of expression and the protection of reputation' (https://bills.parliament.uk/bills/983). The rebalancing was in favour of free expression.

Jack punch Jill, unless you didn't see him punch her and you are under oath in a criminal trial. It is not illegal to tell your neighbours at a party that Jesus loves them. But it is illegal to tell them this by using a loud speaker to broadcast it from your home at 120 decibels at 3 a.m.

Banning incitement, perjury and public nuisance does not ban the expression of an idea in all circumstances, or even in many circumstances. Ideas are implicated in these crimes only under very particular circumstances. That's why these laws do not impede the progress of knowledge or the scrutiny of the powerful. There are plenty of other circumstances in which to get on with those jobs. The threat comes from laws that make it illegal simply to express an idea. No such laws should ever be enacted. This is the rule that legislators and judges should follow.

6 DANGEROUS IDEAS

In March 2019, a gunman murdered 51 people at two mosques in Christchurch, New Zealand. Within weeks of the atrocity, the prime minister, Jacinda Ardern, announced that her government would seek to strengthen New Zealand's hate speech laws, extending the protected groups to include the religious. She has since said that the new legislation may also prohibit hateful speech concerning sexuality, gender, age, disability and employment status. She has even refused to rule out adding political belief to the list.

Never mind if broader hate speech laws would have prevented the Christchurch massacre. For the moment, what matters is only this rationale for them: namely, that the law should prohibit speech that expresses dangerous ideas. An idea is dangerous if it causes people who hear it to do things that are harmful. Hateful statements about Muslims are dangerous because they cause people to hate Muslims and then to murder them. Causing something doesn't mean making it sure to happen. A causes B if A increases the chance of B: that is, if the chance of B is higher with A than without A. Smoking causes lung cancer without raising the chance of it to 100 per cent. Saying hateful things about Muslims increases the chance that the audience will hate Muslims, and hating Muslims increases the chance that you will murder them or harm them in some other way. Saying hateful things about Muslims should therefore be illegal. That's the idea.

This is not the same as a prohibition on inciting murder or other crimes. To be guilty of incitement, you must ask others to commit a crime and you must do so in a context that makes someone's acting upon the request a serious prospect. No such intentions or circumstances are required for hate speech. Nor is hate speech the same as defamation, for two reasons. Whereas you cannot be found guilty of defamation if you can show that what you said is true, there is no 'truth defence' when accused of hate speech. And, in most jurisdictions (though not in England), you can be found guilty of defamation only if some actual harm to the defamed person can be demonstrated. But being guilty of hate speech depends solely on what you said, not on any actual effects of your speech. The rationale for the prohibition is that the speech causes harm. But the prohibition applies directly to the speech, however benign the actual effects of any instance of it.

Hate speech laws are thus a major departure from the uncontroversial restrictions on free speech, such as fraud, perjury and public nuisance, which depend on the time, place and manner of the speech. Whether or not speech is illegally hateful depends solely on the idea expressed. These laws therefore do more to threaten the role of free speech in advancing knowledge than the uncontroversial restrictions do, for the reasons given at the end of chapter 5.

Many will think this is nonsense. 'Hate isn't knowledge' is a nice little slogan they might like. To see why they are wrong, consider research into the biological bases for differences in IQ and, especially, for differences in the average IQs of racial groups and differences in the distribution of IQs among men and women. Some researchers have claimed that, on average, Asians have higher IQs than whites and whites have higher IQs than blacks (see, for example, Rushton and Jenson 2005). They have also found that more men than women occupy the tails of the IQ distribution. In other words, more men than women have very high IQs and very low IQs. And some have claimed that these group differences have biological bases. These ideas are found hateful by many people. Private sector responses mean that publicly expressing them is already a perilous business.[1] There is surely a material chance that hate speech laws will soon be interpreted or amended to prohibit the publication of these ideas, especially when, in English law, the test for whether an action is hateful is simply that someone in the audience believes it is.[2]

---

1 In 2006, Larry Summers lost his job as President of Harvard after claiming that differences in the distribution of IQs among men and women explain why most physics professors are men. In 2019, Noah Carl lost his fellowship at St Edmund's College of Cambridge University for collaborating (on other topics) with people who had conducted research on the connection between race and IQ. To give but two examples of the peril.

2 Racist and religious hate crime – prosecution guidance. Crown Prosecution Service (https://www.cps.gov.uk/legal-guidance/racist-and-religious -hate-crime-prosecution-guidance).

Even if IQ is a bogus concept or the biological theories are false, as many believe (see, for example, Bird 2021), this interpretation of hate speech laws would stifle important research. It would require scientists to suppress certain discoveries, should they make them. And it would discourage scientists from entering the field in the first place. To avoid the risks involved, they will direct their efforts elsewhere. That would be a setback for humanity, since a better understanding of the biological bases of mental function could be a source of untold gains in our well-being.

Or consider the psychology of 'gender identity'. That someone might be wrong about his gender – for example, thinking he is a woman when in fact he is a man – and that his error might be caused by a psychological disorder are considered by many to be hateful ideas. Academics who have published research supporting them have been accused of hate speech.[3] Again, it is easy to imagine the interpretation of hate speech laws coming to cover such publications, which would stifle research that might lead to important discoveries.

Set aside hate speech laws for a moment and consider the justification for them that we are considering in this section: namely, that they prevent the expression of dangerous ideas. Big new ideas will often strike people as dangerous. By the mid nineteenth century, most scientists agreed that we humans are descended from more primitive primates and, ultimately, from even more

---

3 Reader outcry prompts Brown to retract press release on trans teens. Retraction Watch (https://retractionwatch.com/2018/08/29/reader-out cry-prompts-brown-to-retract-press-release-on-trans-teens/).

primitive life-forms, such as fish. Charles Darwin's contribution was to show that evolution and the adaptation of species to their environments resulted from the unconscious process of natural selection. This undermined the myth that humans occupy a special God-given place in the cosmos, outside the rest of nature. Many railed against the theory, not only as heretical nonsense but as socially catastrophic. It would make people wicked, because moral behaviour, they believed, depends on believing the Christian myth of mankind's relationship with God. The philosopher Daniel Dennett's book on 'evolution and the meanings of life' (its subtitle) is entitled *Darwin's Dangerous Idea* (Dennett 1996). Had the expression of dangerous ideas been prohibited in mid-nineteenth-century England, perhaps by a law prohibiting speech that 'threatens our way of life' (as the 2021 Online Safety Bill proposes), Darwin's 1859 *On the Origin of Species* might not have been published. Indeed, he might not have conducted the research behind it. That would have been a serious setback for the progress of knowledge.

Of course, the Christian moralists were wrong. Moral behaviour does not require a religious worldview, and morals have not collapsed since Darwin's ideas became widely believed. But that is irrelevant. Had a law preventing dangerous speech then prevailed, it would probably have been taken to rule out the expression of Darwin's theory of natural selection. Why should we believe that prohibitions on dangerous speech, however realised in law, will not nowadays stifle the expression of important new ideas?

It is impossible to know the long-term cost of slowing the advance of knowledge. After all, we don't know what we don't know. Nor, therefore, do we know how valuable this knowledge would be to us. Or, to put it the other way around, we don't know the loss from not having it. But the gains from the rapid advance of knowledge over the past five hundred years have been so great that we must presume the loss to be very large. Nothing matters as much for human welfare as knowledge, and nothing has produced knowledge as effectively as free inquiry unconstrained by authority.

But what if a speech prohibition undermines free inquiry just a little bit? Then the benefits of the prohibition might well exceed the losses that come from impeding inquiry. No they won't. Not only can undermining free inquiry 'just a little bit' be very costly but, as I will argue in chapter 8, undermining free inquiry just a little bit is likely to lead to undermining it quite a lot. And, as I will argue here, the benefits from prohibiting dangerous speech are negligible.

I cannot argue this by showing where those who favour some prohibition on dangerous speech go wrong when estimating its benefits. For they make no such estimations. Jacinda Ardern did not when recommending hate speech laws as a way of stopping murder motivated by religious hatred. Nor did the Royal Commission of Inquiry that investigated the Christchurch massacre and endorsed Ardern's proposal. Nor did the UK government when making the case for its Online Safety Bill. Nor does Cass Sunstein (the famous Harvard law professor) in his 2021 book *Liars* when arguing for laws prohibiting the dissemination of dangerous falsehoods. This is a serious defect in their arguments. Since they wish to limit our freedom, the onus is on them to show that doing so will deliver great benefits. Why do they not even try?

One possibility is that they do not genuinely seek to minimise net harm but merely wish to ban speech they don't like. A serious attempt to estimate harm reduction might not deliver the desired result. Perhaps. But, of course, I cannot know what they genuinely seek. Another possibility is that they think it simply obvious that their prohibitions will bestow great benefits on the population. Trying to estimate the benefits would be a waste of precious intellectual energy. If so, they are overconfident.

A question that ought to trouble anyone who thinks that hateful speech causes murder is why there are so few murders of people spoken about hatefully. Let's stick with Muslims. Though it is illegal in the UK to incite hatred on the basis of religion, speech contemptuous of Islam and of Muslims abounds.[4] Anyone so inclined could easily find some nasty anti-Muslim material on the Internet. And most of us who are not so inclined will have occasionally heard Muslims spoken of hatefully. Yet, in the last twenty years, only four Muslims in the UK have been murdered by someone motivated by anti-Muslim hatred.[5]

---

4   The UK law against inciting racial or religious hatred sets a high threshold – requiring the intention or likelihood of stirring up hatred – which much speech contemptuous of races or religions passes beneath.

5   List of Islamophobic incidents (https://en.wikipedia.org/wiki/List_of_Is lamophobic_incidents#United_Kingdom).

At most, anti-Muslim hate speech each year turns only 0.0000003 per cent of the British population into Muslim killers.[6] Why does it have such a tiny effect?

Part of the answer is that inspiring a murderous level of hatred isn't that easy. The first step in the causal chain – from hate speech to murderous hatred – very rarely happens. The other part of the answer is that murder is illegal. I don't want to murder anyone. But even if I did, I wouldn't do it. The prospect of being caught and imprisoned deters me. The same goes for other crimes (which I also do not want to commit!). A causal chain from action A to bad outcome B does not warrant the prohibition of A if something else already stops B from happening.

Of course, the threat of detection and punishment is not a perfect deterrent to crime. Murder is illegal, but murders still happen. Other crimes, with lesser penalties, are even more common. That's why it makes sense also to criminalise things that greatly increase the chance of crime and have little independent value – inciting crime and conspiring to commit crimes being the obvious examples. Deterrence is extended at no social cost. But, as noted, hate speech does not much increase the chance of crime. So criminalising it cannot be justified on this ground, especially when potentially valuable speech is likely to get caught in the net of hate speech laws.

I cannot leave the matter here, however, because preventing crimes is not the goal of all those who want to

---

6   0.0000003 per cent = 4 (the number of murders) ÷ 20 (the number of years covered) ÷ 70,000,000 (the population of the UK).

prohibit speech they consider hateful. It isn't the goal of the eminent political philosopher Jeremy Waldron, for example. In his 2012 book, *The Harm in Hate Speech*, Waldron argues that hate speech should be illegal because it is a kind of 'group libel' that harms the 'dignity' of the group's members. By dignity, Waldron means 'the social standing, the fundamentals of basic reputation that entitle [people] to be treated as equals in the ordinary operations of society' (Waldron 2012: 5). Hate speech laws, Waldron argues, provide a public good: namely, the 'visible assurance of just treatment that a society is supposed to provide to all of its members' (ibid.: 81).

Waldron is right about the phenomenon. Members of vilified groups suffer a degradation of their social standing and their ability to go about their lives in public. Not long ago in America, blacks and Jews were openly called sub-human, parasites, diseased, among other things. It was common in Britain in the mid twentieth century, and still happens occasionally today, for people to yell 'go home Paki!' at South Asians.

These dreadful facts do not, however, justify hate speech laws. In part, this is because much of the abusive speech Waldron wants eliminated is already illegal. It is a crime in America (which is Waldron's concern) to directly threaten or intimidate someone and it is a misdemeanour to taunt, insult or challenge someone 'with purpose to harass'.[7] Of course, as it stands, US law doesn't prohibit the expression of hateful ideas when

---

7   US Model Penal Code §22 and §240.

they are not threats, harassment or the like – not, for example, when they are expressed in a newspaper column or in a pamphlet distributed on the street.[8] But nor should it. For, as noted above, important ideas may be deemed hateful by the authorities. And their suppression may slow the advance of knowledge or the scrutiny of politically powerful groups.[9]

Governments can provide the 'assurance of just treatment' sought by Waldron without the suppression of otherwise legal speech. Most obviously, they can simply provide just treatment. They can give the members of all groups the right to vote, equal protection of the law, equal entitlements to state education, state pensions, state healthcare, and so on. The social standing of black Americans has improved greatly over the last two centuries. President Lyndon Johnson justified the 1964 Civil Rights Act by claiming that 'a man has a right not to be insulted in front of his children'. No such right exists, of course. But that isn't to the present point, which is that the Civil Rights Act provided the assurance sought by Waldron without introducing hate speech laws or otherwise overturning the First Amendment. The standing of

---

8   Waldron approves of the anomalous US Supreme Court case, *Beauharnais v. Illinois* (1952), in which the court approved of the doctrine of group libel with respect to racist pamphlets circulated in Chicago.

9   Leiter (2012) points out that in India 'Hindus, who were indeed the target of institutionalized denigration during the colonial period, have used their political power, once India was independent, to impose restrictions on the portrayal of Hinduism that went well beyond "hate speech" to encompass scholarly discussion of Hinduism that does not comport with the understanding of right-wing Hindus'.

Jews and homosexuals has also improved, again, without the help of speech laws.[10]

Waldron is not the only eminent scholar who favours speech restrictions aimed at preventing harms that are not illegal. Cass Sunstein does too. In *Liars*, he proposes that the regulation of speech should be guided by the following principle (Sunstein 2021: 72):

> False statements should be constitutionally protected unless the government can show that they threaten to cause serious harm that cannot be avoided through a more speech-protective route.

The serious harms he is referring to are not crimes. Among other things, Sunstein is worried about people's health being harmed by getting false ideas: for example, that smoking doesn't cause cancer or that Covid-19 is a hoax (ibid.: 106). And he is worried about political harm being caused by false ideas, such as the idea that Hillary Clinton is less than perfectly honest (ibid.: 74).[11] Sunstein does not, in the end, favour legal prohibitions on expressing these opinions, preferring other devices in the government's 'large and growing toolbox', such as requiring social media sites to point out that they are false (ibid.: 133). But that is

---

10 For other critiques of Waldron (2012), see Leiter (2012) and Heinze (2016).

11 In case readers suspect I am misrepresenting Sunstein regarding Clinton, I quote: 'It follows that if you are told that some public official is a liar and a crook, you might continue to believe that, in some part of your mind, even if you know that she is perfectly honest. (In 2016, the sustained attacks on Hillary Clinton worked for this reason, even when people were aware they were lies.)'

not the present issue, which is the legality of the speech-caused harms he is concerned to avoid. Smoking, refusing a Covid vaccination and voting for Donald Trump instead of Hillary Clinton are not crimes. So I cannot argue that, for the purpose of avoiding these harms, speech prohibitions (or other devices from the government's toolbox) are redundant.

But I don't need to. The idea that the government should prohibit or otherwise interfere with false speech that has harmful political outcomes faces two serious objections. The first is that it requires government officials to decide which political outcomes are harmful. Most Democrats genuinely believe that a Republican president will harm society. And most Republicans believe that a Democrat president will harm society. Suppose the Democrats are correct. Then false statements that promote the Republican candidate should be prohibited (or officially corrected) while false statements that promote the Democrat candidate should be protected by the First Amendment. For, on Sunstein's principle, '[w]hen falsehoods are banned, it is not only because they are falsehoods but also because they threaten to cause real harm'.

Of course, it may be the Democrat president who will cause more harm if elected. The harm arbiters will need to decide. And there's the problem. Giving government officials the power to make this decision looks like an invitation to rig politics in favour of whoever is currently in power, and thereby to undermine the constraint that free speech places on would-be tyrants. The government-determined good side is free to lie, while the government-determined bad side is allowed to say only what the government says is true.

Which brings us to the second objection to Sunstein's principle. It requires government officials to decide what is true and what is false. Unlike the matter of which outcomes are harmful, on which Sunstein seems to think there can be no serious doubt, he does acknowledge that government officials might not always know what is true and what is false. Indeed, he acknowledges that they might say that something is true even when they know it isn't because saying so serves their purposes (ibid.: 56). But don't worry. The truth will not be determined by government officials. It will be determined by an 'independent tribunal [of judges who have] concluded that there is no reasonable doubt on the matter' (ibid.: 60). The history of what judges have concluded is beyond reasonable doubt does not inspire complete confidence in this proposal. But the more compelling objection is Sunstein's remarkable political naivety. Can he seriously doubt that the independence of a tribunal with such astonishing political influence would not soon be subverted?

The Online Safety Bill, now before the UK parliament, aims to achieve Sunstein's goal. It imposes a legal obligation (a 'duty of care') on online platforms, such as Facebook and Twitter, to remove speech that is harmful misinformation. Enforcing this law will require the regulator, Ofcom, to decide which outcomes are harmful and which ideas are false. To avoid the massive penalties threatened by the Bill, up to 10 per cent of the company's global revenue, online companies will try to anticipate which ideas Ofcom's bureaucrats will deem harmful falsehoods and design automated techniques for removing them. By expressing their opinions, bureaucrats at Ofcom will be able to exert great influence over which ideas get expressed online. And the bureaucrats at Ofcom, of course, will be keen to please the politicians on whom their jobs and powers depend.

Political speech can be dangerous. As noted in chapter 4, voters are ignorant and inclined to certain errors. When presented with falsehoods, they may well believe them and end up voting for the wrong candidate or making other mistakes, such as not taking vaccines that are in fact safe. But any attempt to prevent this by banning the expression of dangerous falsehoods will be worse than the problem it is supposed to solve. It will allow those in power to hijack public discussion and limit the scrutiny and criticism to which they are exposed.

7 OFFENSIVE IDEAS

In the previous chapter I considered speech laws as a way of preventing the expression of dangerous ideas, ideas that cause people to do illegal or otherwise harmful things. But that isn't their only rationale. Some support speech laws as a way of preventing harm that speech inflicts directly on its audience. The harm they have in mind is psychological. They aim to prevent not damage to bodies or property but to feelings. More specifically, they favour speech laws as a way of protecting people from hearing things that they find offensive.

As with prohibitions on the expression of dangerous ideas, prohibitions on the expression of offensive ideas fail my test. They inhibit the growth of knowledge and scrutiny of the powerful. Before explaining why, however, I want to cast doubt on the idea that offensive speech causes harm.

My reason is not that I agree with those who think that offence is not harm because it involves no physical or financial injury. It is quite possible to suffer purely psychological harms. For example, if I spike your drink with a drug that gives you terrifying hallucinations, I harm you.

Benefit and harm should be understood in terms of someone's willingness to pay. Something is good for you (beneficial) if you would be willing to pay for it. Something is bad for you (harmful) if you would pay to avoid it. Payment needn't be in money. When I spend an hour preparing my dinner, that shows that the meal benefits me. Nor need paying for the desired outcome be possible. No payment, monetary or other, will stop the rain from falling. Still, the difference between rain that benefits me and rain that harms me is that I would pay for the former and pay to avoid the latter, if only I could.

With this understanding of harm, it should be clear that offensive behaviour can harm its audience. Openly masturbating on a crowded bus, for example. I, for one, would get off at the first stop and wait for the next bus. That's a way of paying to stop witnessing the offensive behaviour. Offensive speech can also harm its audience. Hearing disparaging remarks about people you love, for example, can be upsetting. The feelings induced can be sufficiently unpleasant that, if it were possible, you would pay to be rid of them.

But just because offence *can be* harm, that doesn't mean it always really *is* harm. Consider physical pain during sex. This would harm most people. They would pay to avoid it. But not sexual masochists. They would pay to experience it, and some of them do in fact pay money for it. When a masochist is involved, pain during sex is not harmful. Similarly, some people – 'offence masochists', as I will call them – enjoy being offended. You can tell they do because they actively seek out the source of their offence. Having found it, they complain loudly and protest against the villainy of the speaker. But all that angry noise is no more proof of harm than is the whimpering of the sexual masochist who will be returning to the brothel next week with his wallet at the ready. Nor does my shouting at the TV news mean that it is harming me. I am having a ball! That's why I keep watching it and keep yelling at it. And that's why the speech masochist keeps following Jordan Peterson on Twitter, or whoever it is whose opinions bother him so much.

The existence of a discrete BDSM brothel is not a source of harm because no one who dislikes the pain dished out would visit the brothel. Similarly, the existence of Dave Chappelle's Netflix comedy special is not a source of harm because no one who dislikes his jokes about trans people would watch the show. If someone offended by such jokes nevertheless chooses to watch it, chances are he's an offence masochist.

Much of the current anxiety about offensive speech concerns the Internet. But little could be easier than avoiding offensive speech online. Here's a simple way. Don't go online. Of course, that will be too great a loss to most people. So here is another way. Don't follow people on social media whose views you find offensive. Ease of avoidance is the principle that guides current law regarding grossly offensive behaviour. Masturbating on a bus is illegal because those who are offended by it cannot easily avoid the sight of you doing it. Masturbating in your bedroom is not illegal because anyone who sees it must have gone out of their way to get a glimpse.

Of course, some will claim that they are offended not by viewing Dave Chappelle's transphobic comedy special (they wouldn't dream of watching it!) but by knowing that others are watching it and laughing at it. Its existence offends them. Similarly, some might say that it is not the sight of someone masturbating in his bedroom that offends them (they wouldn't dream of looking!) but the simple fact that it is going on.

How much harm is the knowledge of such facts doing to the offended? In theory, this is measured by what they are willing to pay to avoid it – which, in this case, requires the offending facts to be abolished. In practice, however, their willingness to pay will be difficult to observe. Those offended by Chappelle's transphobic jokes might be able to club together and raise enough money to pay him to stop making them. But paying Chappelle to stop making transphobic jokes would only encourage other comedians to do so. So Chappelle won't be paid to keep quiet. And where private conduct is concerned, there's a confirmation problem. You could pay a young man £50 a week not to masturbate in private but it will be difficult to know if he is honouring his side of the bargain. For this reason, no one would make the offer.

When we cannot observe what those offended by the mere existence of things actually pay to eliminate them, we cannot know what they are willing to pay. Words are cheap. Whatever they say about their misery, what they would pay to be rid of its cause may be a pittance. Indeed, we cannot know that those offended by the mere existence of something are not also offence masochists. Just as some people enjoy being offended by listening to Chappelle's transphobic jokes, some might enjoy being offended by knowing that they exist. Contemplating the sinfulness of the world was an enjoyable pastime for nineteenth-century Christian moralists. Why assume that contemporary moralists enjoy it any less? But, then, if we don't know whether this kind of offence is net-harmful or net-beneficial, we cannot give any weight to it when deciding which speech should be allowed.

In short, it is unclear what problem prohibitions on the expression of offensive ideas are supposed to solve. The ease with which most offensive speech can be avoided means that most offence is taken voluntarily and is not therefore harmful. And offensive speech that cannot easily be avoided by its audience – such as profane billboards erected near a church or obscenities yelled into someone's face – is already prohibited by other laws, such as those concerning obscenity and harassment.[1] We have no reason to believe that society suffers from an excess of offensive speech. In fact, for all we know, offence masochism may be such a common character trait that society would benefit from increasing the quantity of offensive speech.

Laws aimed specifically at prohibiting offensive speech are not merely unnecessary. They are harmful. They threaten to interfere with free inquiry and to constrain scrutiny of the powerful. This is because they do not make illegality depend on the time, place and manner of the speech. Except when said in private, the simple expression of some ideas is made illegal.[2]

---

1 In 2016, the 4th U.S. Circuit Court of Appeals upheld a South Carolina law that prohibited profanity near a church or school.

2 In March 2021, the Scottish parliament passed the Hate Crime and Public Order (Scotland) Bill into law. It makes hateful speech a criminal offence even when uttered in the privacy of the family home.

In chapter 6, I explained how hate speech laws – whether motivated by a desire to limit dangerous speech or offensive speech or both – could easily impede free inquiry. The same goes for any law that aims to prohibit the expression of offensive ideas. Big new ideas are likely to be considered not only dangerous but offensive. In the nineteenth century, it was Christian sensibilities that were offended by new ideas. Darwin's dangerous idea was also an offensive idea. Nowadays the sensibilities that get offended tend to concern issues of 'identity': gender, sexuality, race and nationality, among others. A nineteenth-century Christian offended by the idea that he is descended from a fish would probably have been surprised to learn that in the twenty-first century people will be offended by the idea that women do not have penises. But some are. And they still would be even if women really don't have penises, just as humans really are descended from fish but that didn't stop many nineteenth-century Christians being offended by the idea. What offends people and what is false are connected only loosely, if at all. So laws that aim to prevent the simple expression of offensive ideas are always liable to impede the growth of knowledge. Letting sensibilities unconnected to error constrain what can be said is no way to promote the truth.

Nor will it help to hold the powerful to account. Iran is a theocracy. The ayatollahs who run the country claim to be executing Allah's will. Their legitimacy would be undermined if Iranians came to the view, now common in the West, that Allah does not exist. But expressing this idea is illegal in Iran. This protects Iranians' religious sensibilities from being offended. It also protects the rule of the ayatollahs.

Offensive ideas are no less politically relevant in Western countries. Bryan Caplan has (almost) written a book in which he argues, among other things, that the poor in rich countries only have themselves to blame (Caplan, forthcoming). This is a politically important idea because it might show that current policies aimed at reducing poverty are misguided. But it is also an offensive idea. For many, the idea that the poor are victims of society or of the rich is close to a sacred article of faith. Denying it is as offensive to them as denying the existence of Allah is to an ayatollah.

Expressing Caplan's idea is not now prohibited by any speech law, including the UK's hate speech laws. But it is easy to imagine the characteristics protected by hate speech law being extended to include socio-economic status or 'employment status', as is a genuine prospect under New Zealand's proposed hate speech legislation. Saying that those who are poor or unemployed brought this misfortune on themselves would surely then violate the law. Publishing Caplan's book would be illegal. And the politicians who promote policies premised on the poor being victims of society rather than of themselves would be relieved of the need to respond to a bothersome line of criticism.

Or consider Israel. Some commentators now claim that anti-Zionism – that is, opposition to the existence of a Jewish state – is anti-Semitic. If so, arguing against the existence of a Jewish state may well violate the law against inciting religious hatred. That is not how the authorities now interpret anti-Zionist speech but, again, it isn't hard to imagine. Then Zionist politicians would enjoy a reduction in the sources of criticism they face.

8   WHY BE UNCOMPROMISING?

As the philosopher J. L. Austin pointed out, you can do things with words (Austin 1962). You can flatter, flirt, insult, incite, betray, defraud, marry and much besides. And many of the things you can do with words are illegal, such as inciting murder and defrauding customers. The law properly prohibits speech that commits these crimes. But these are not *speech laws*, any more than the law against assault is a punching law. Punching is illegal when it is assault but not otherwise – not when keeping fit in a boxing class, for example. Similarly, saying that you saw Jack rob Jill is illegal when it is perjury but not when it is a true revelation in a memoir. Speech laws, as I have been using the expression, ban the mere expression of an idea. The clearest examples are laws, common among European countries, that prohibit Holocaust denial. The crime depends solely on the idea expressed. Hate speech laws are the same. The criminality arises from the hatefulness of the idea itself, not from any other criminal activity in which the expression of the idea is implicated. We should have no such laws because they threaten free inquiry and the political scrutiny that prevents tyranny. That's the principle that should guide legislators and judges.

But am I not being absurdly rigid and doctrinaire? The law banning Holocaust denial in France has not led to tyranny or constrained research. Am I not indulging in an absurd 'slippery slope argument'?

To see why not, the first step is recognising that slippery slope arguments are not always fallacious. Imagine a nineteenth-century Christian at a church meeting who says that slavery should be abolished because all humans should be free to associate as they please. 'No, no, no!' the vicar tells her: 'accept that principle and soon homosexuals will be getting married'. The vicar was right, not only in logic but as a matter of political fact. The liberal principles that count against slavery also count against prohibitions on gay marriage. And the political dynamics set in play by policies premised on liberal principles led to a cascade of liberal policies. In the last two hundred years we have moved along a slippery slope of liberalism (which shows that you can slip up slopes as well as down).

Slippage is likely in the absence of a 'limiting principle'. In 1985, a Private Member's Bill in the New Zealand parliament sought to repeal the law against homosexuality. It sparked a great public debate on the issue. A friend of mine complained about the proposal on the ground that it would end up with him being forced to engage in homosexual sex. It was a silly objection because the principle invoked to justify legalising homosexuality was that personal choice should be respected, which also justifies the prohibition on rape. There was no good argument from one to the other. And, indeed, the legalisation of homosexuality has not led to the legalisation of rape. The politics followed the logic.

The problem with speech laws is the absence of a limiting principle. The law against inciting murder is a self-limiting restriction on speech. If speech isn't credibly incitement to murder, and not much is, it won't be penalised (under this law). A law against expressing false ideas does not similarly constrain the authorities. What controversial idea cannot be cast as false by a government with an interest in doing so? As US Supreme Court justices put it in their judgement on *United States v. Alvarez*, a famous First Amendment case:

> Permitting the government to decree this speech a criminal offence, whether shouted from the rooftop or made in a barely audible whisper, would endorse government authority to compile a list of subjects about which false statements are punishable. *That governmental power has no limiting principle*. Our constitutional tradition stands against the idea that we need Oceania's Ministry of Truth [my italics].

The same goes for prohibiting dangerous or offensive speech. No clear limit is imposed on the speech that politicians might criminalise. Almost any intellectually or politically significant speech could plausibly be taken to be dangerous or offensive. The principle that expressing dangerous or offensive ideas should be illegal places politicians at the top of a steep slope.

That's why the criminalisation of Holocaust denial is not as harmless as it may seem. The content of the law creates no slippery slope. It prohibits the expression of just one idea. Although a Frenchman may not deny that the Nazis murdered millions of Jews, he may quite legally deny any other historic atrocity. But the principle justifying the Holocaust denial law – preventing the expression of harmful ideas – provides no limitation. It is only an arbitrary application of the principle that explains why denying the Holocaust is illegal but denying other genocides is not. Unsurprisingly, the French government is lobbied to prohibit the denial of other historic events, such as the alleged 1915 genocide of Armenians at the hands of Turks.[1] Also unsurprisingly, it has passed laws that give it considerable powers to demand the removal of content from online platforms. The French government is slipping down the slope that the law against Holocaust denial puts it on. They are following the logic of that law, a logic which provides no clear stopping point. Similarly, the Online Safety Bill merely adds to the UK laws that ban the expression of ideas deemed harmful by the authorities. No implicit or explicit principle in the law-making process provides any reason to believe that this will be the last such law. On the contrary, the rationale for the law gives us reason to expect more of its kind.

Whenever democratic politicians propose or pass speech laws, they reaffirm their commitment to freedom of speech and open political debate. 'Don't worry, censorship is safe in our hands'. This isn't good enough. 'Trust me' is not a limiting principle. Of course, sometimes we should

---

1   Denying the Armenian genocide was illegal in France from 2015 until 2017, when the constitutional court overturned the law.

trust people who don't offer one. I trust my friends not to go too far in their teasing jokes, even though they have articulated no limiting principle. But I do not trust those who wield the coercive power of the state not to go too far in their regulation of speech. Why should I when speech that benefits society can harm them?

Speech prohibitions imposed by the rulers of distant societies, such as seventeenth-century Roman Catholic Europe and modern-day Iran and China, invariably strike modern Westerners as oppressive, as harming the population for the benefit of the rulers. The justifications offered by the rulers, usually that the censorship will protect society from harm, strike us as laughably implausible and self-serving. But when it comes to our own societies and our own rulers, we are less sceptical. Perhaps this is because authoritarian rulers are always at least partly in tune with their populations. They ban speech that many in the population also dislike. The speech prohibitions of Iran and China probably look better to the populations of those countries than they do to us. But this should only encourage us to step back and look at the big historical picture. When those in power seek to control the ideas we can hear, they are up to no good, even when they honestly believe they are doing God's work. It is all too easy for the kind of people who get to the top in politics to believe that their interests and the nation's interests are one and the same. A speech prohibition that eases their maintenance of power or the progress of their policy agenda must thereby benefit the population.

Stopping them from indulging such delusions requires commitment to a limiting principle on legislation that restricts speech. The law should never prohibit speech solely because of what is said. No ideas should be illegal. Those who can constrain the government – judges, members of parliament, journalists and, ultimately, voters – must resist the imposition of such laws. And the resistance must be uncompromising.

REFERENCES

Austin, J. (1962) *How to Do Things with Words.* Oxford University Press.

Bird, K. (2021) No support for the hereditarian hypothesis of the Black–White achievement gap using polygenic scores and tests for divergent selection. *American Journal of Physical Anthropology* 175(2): 465–76.

Brennan, G. and Lomasky, L. (1993) *Democracy and Decision: The Pure Theory of Electoral Preference.* Cambridge University Press.

Butler, E. (2012) *Public Choice: A Primer.* London: Institute for Economic Affairs.

Caplan, B. (2008) *The Myth of the Rational Voter: Why Democracies Choose Bad Policies.* Princeton University Press.

Caplan, B. (forthcoming) *Poverty: Who to Blame.*

Condorcet, Marquis de (1785) *Essay on the Application of Analysis to the Probability of Majority Decisions.*

Davies, S. (2019) *The Wealth Explosion: The Nature and Origins of Modernity.* London: Edward Everett Root.

Dennett, D. C. (1996) *Darwin's Dangerous Idea: Evolution and the Meanings of Life.* London: Penguin.

Downs, A. (1957) *An Economic Theory of Democracy.* New York: Harper and Row.

Feeney, M. (2021) Are social media companies common carriers? Cato at Liberty (https://www.cato.org/blog/are-social-media -companies-common-carriers).

Feinberg, J. (1985) *Offense to Others*. Oxford University Press.

Hammer, P. (1988) Note: Free speech and the 'acid bath': an evaluation and critique of Judge Richard Posner's economic interpretation of the First Amendment. *Michigan Law Review* 87(2): 499–536.

Heinze, E. (2016) *Hate Speech and Democratic Citizenship*. Oxford University Press.

Howard, J. (2019) Free speech and hate speech. *Annual Review of Political Science* 22: 93–109.

Leiter, B. (2012) Waldron on the regulation of hate speech. *Notre Dame Philosophical Reviews* (https://ndpr.nd.edu/reviews/the -harm-in-hate-speech/).

McCloskey, D. (2017) *Bourgeois Equality: How Ideas, Not Capital or Institutions, Enriched the World*. Chicago University Press.

Milton, J. (1644) *Areopagitica*. Reprinted in Milton, J. (2014) *Areopagitica and Other Writings*. London: Penguin

Mokyr, J. (2017) *A Culture of Growth: The Origins of the Modern Economy*. Princeton University Press.

Posner, R. (1986) Free speech in an economic perspective. *Suffolk University Law Review* 20(1): 1–54.

Rauch, J. (1993) *Kindly Inquisitors: The New Attacks on Free Thought*. Chicago University Press.

Ridley, M. (2020) *How Innovation Works*. New York: Fourth Estate.

Rushton, J. and Jenson, A. (2005) Thirty years of research on race differences in cognitive ability. *Psychology, Public Policy, and Law* 11(2): 235–94.

Sunstein, C. (2021) *Liars: Falsehoods and Free Speech in an Age of Deception.* Oxford University Press.

Thaler, R. and Sunstein, C. (2008) *Nudge: Improving Decisions about Health, Wealth and Happiness.* London: Penguin.

Waldron, J. (2012) *The Harm in Hate Speech.* Cambridge, MA: Harvard University Press.

Warburton, N. (2009) *Free Speech: A Very Short Introduction.* Oxford University Press.

ABOUT THE IEA

The Institute is a research and educational charity (No. CC 235 351), limited by guarantee. Its mission is to improve understanding of the fundamental institutions of a free society by analysing and expounding the role of markets in solving economic and social problems.

The IEA achieves its mission by:

- a high-quality publishing programme
- conferences, seminars, lectures and other events
- outreach to school and college students
- brokering media introductions and appearances

The IEA, which was established in 1955 by the late Sir Antony Fisher, is an educational charity, not a political organisation. It is independent of any political party or group and does not carry on activities intended to affect support for any political party or candidate in any election or referendum, or at any other time. It is financed by sales of publications, conference fees and voluntary donations.

In addition to its main series of publications, the IEA also publishes (jointly with the University of Buckingham), *Economic Affairs*.

The IEA is aided in its work by a distinguished international Academic Advisory Council and an eminent panel of Honorary Fellows. Together with other academics, they review prospective IEA publications, their comments being passed on anonymously to authors. All IEA papers are therefore subject to the same rigorous independent refereeing process as used by leading academic journals.

IEA publications enjoy widespread classroom use and course adoptions in schools and universities. They are also sold throughout the world and often translated/reprinted.

Since 1974 the IEA has helped to create a worldwide network of 100 similar institutions in over 70 countries. They are all independent but share the IEA's mission.

Views expressed in the IEA's publications are those of the authors, not those of the Institute (which has no corporate view), its Managing Trustees, Academic Advisory Council members or senior staff.

Members of the Institute's Academic Advisory Council, Honorary Fellows, Trustees and Staff are listed on the following page.

The Institute gratefully acknowledges financial support for its publications programme and other work from a generous benefaction by the late Professor Ronald Coase.

Socialism: The Failed Idea That Never Dies
Kristian Niemietz
ISBN 978-0-255-36770-7; £17.50

Top Dogs and Fat Cats: The Debate on High Pay
Edited by J. R. Shackleton
ISBN 978-0-255-36773-8; £15.00

School Choice around the World … And the Lessons We Can Learn
Edited by Pauline Dixon and Steve Humble
ISBN 978-0-255-36779-0; £15.00

School of Thought: 101 Great Liberal Thinkers
Eamonn Butler
ISBN 978-0-255-36776-9; £12.50

Raising the Roof: How to Solve the United Kingdom's Housing Crisis
Edited by Jacob Rees-Mogg and Radomir Tylecote
ISBN 978-0-255-36782-0; £12.50

How Many Light Bulbs Does It Take to Change the World?
Matt Ridley and Stephen Davies
ISBN 978-0-255-36785-1; £10.00

The Henry Fords of Healthcare … Lessons the West Can Learn from the East
Nima Sanandaji
ISBN 978-0-255-36788-2; £10.00

An Introduction to Entrepreneurship
Eamonn Butler
ISBN 978-0-255-36794-3; £12.50

An Introduction to Democracy
Eamonn Butler
ISBN 978-0-255-36797-4; £12.50

Having Your Say: Threats to Free Speech in the 21st Century
Edited by J. R. Shackleton
ISBN 978-0-255-36800-1; £17.50

The Sharing Economy: Its Pitfalls and Promises
Michael C. Munger
ISBN 978-0-255-36791-2; £12.50

An Introduction to Trade and Globalisation
Eamonn Butler
ISBN 978-0-255-36803-2; £12.50

Other IEA publications

Comprehensive information on other publications and the wider work of the IEA can be found at www.iea.org.uk. To order any publication please see below.

Personal customers

Orders from personal customers should be directed to the IEA:

IEA
2 Lord North Street
FREEPOST LON10168
London SW1P 3YZ
Tel: 020 7799 8911, Fax: 020 7799 2137
Email: sales@iea.org.uk

Trade customers

All orders from the book trade should be directed to the IEA's distributor:

NBN International (IEA Orders)
Orders Dept.
NBN International
10 Thornbury Road
Plymouth PL6 7PP
Tel: 01752 202301, Fax: 01752 202333
Email: orders@nbninternational.com

IEA subscriptions

The IEA also offers a subscription service to its publications. For a single annual payment (currently £42.00 in the UK), subscribers receive every monograph the IEA publishes. For more information please contact:

Subscriptions
IEA
2 Lord North Street
FREEPOST LON10168
London SW1P 3YZ
Tel: 020 7799 8911, Fax: 020 7799 2137
Email: accounts@iea.org.uk